Caring for Your
Guinea Pig

Jill Foran

Weigl Publishers Inc.

Project Coordinator
Heather C. Hudak

Design and Layout
Warren Clark
Katherine Phillips

Copy Editor
Tina Schwartzenberger

Photo Research
Tracey Carruthers

Locate the guinea pig paw prints throughout the book to find useful tips on caring for your pet.

Published by Weigl Publishers Inc.
350 5th Avenue, Suite 3304, PMB 6G
New York, NY 10118-0069 USA
Web site: www.weigl.com

Library of Congress Cataloging-in-Publication Data

Foran, Jill.
  Caring for your guinea pig / Jill Foran.
     v. cm. -- (Caring for your pet)
Contents: Guinea pigs pals -- Guinea pig profiles -- Crazy for cavies -- Life cycle -- Picking your pet -- Guinea pig gear -- Getting to know your guinea pig -- Guinea pigging out -- Keeping clean -- Staying healthy -- Making friends with your guinea pig -- Best in show.
  ISBN 1-59036-116-4 (lib. bdg. : alk. paper)
 1. Guinea pigs as pets--Juvenile literature. [1. Guinea pigs. 2. Pets.] I. Title. II. Caring for your pet (Mankato, Minn.)
  SF459.G9F67 2004
  636.9'3592--dc21

                        2003001383

Printed in the United States of America
1 2 3 4 5 6 7 8 9 0   07 06 05 04 03

Photograph and Text Credits
Every reasonable effort has been made to trace ownership and to obtain permission to reprint copyright material. The publishers would be pleased to have any errors or omissions brought to their attention so that they may be corrected in subsequent printings.

Cover: Abyssinian (Norvia Behling/ Behling and Johnson); **Norvia Behling/Behling and Johnson**: pages 4, 11 top, 11 bottom, 12, 13, 14, 16, 17, 27, 30, 31; **Gerry Bucsis & Barbara Somerville**: pages 6 left, 6 right, 7 middle, 8, 25 top, 28; **Diane Calkins/Click the Photo Connection**; pages 3, 6 middle, 7 left, 7 right, 9, 10 bottom, 15, 20, 21, 24, 25 bottom; **COMSTOCK, Inc.**: pages 18/19; **Hammytime Publishing**: page 26; **Tina Schwartzenberger**: page 5; **Rosemary Shelton/Click the Photo Connection**: page 23; **Connie Summers/Behling and Johnson**: title page, 10 top, 22.

King-Smith, Dick and Brian Floca (illustrator). *Jenius: The Amazing Guinea Pig.* New York: Hyperion Books for Children, 1996.

Contents

Guinea Pig Pals

Guinea pigs make great pets. Their cute faces, pudgy bodies, and gentle nature have made them popular household companions in many parts of the world. Not only are guinea pigs cute, they are easy to care for. They are clean and quiet, and do not require much space. Guinea pigs have very good **temperaments**. They are not likely to bite their handlers, and they usually do not climb or chew.

■ Guinea pigs are great pets for children. Guinea pigs need less care than dogs and provide much affection.

Although guinea pigs are good natured, looking after them is a big responsibility. Once you have a pet guinea pig, you must take care of him every day. You must give him what he needs to live a happy and healthy life. Guinea pigs require a balanced diet, lots of exercise, and plenty of attention. If you give your pet the love and care he needs, he will return your love.

■ When your guinea pig squeaks or coos, it means he is happy.

Fascinating Facts

- Guinea pigs are not related to pigs. They belong to the rodent group, which also includes chinchillas, gerbils, hamsters, mice, porcupines, and rats.
- Another name for a guinea pig is cavy. The name cavy comes from the scientific term *Cavia porcellus*. Guinea pigs belong to the *Cavia porcellus* species.

Pet Profiles

There are thirteen **breeds** of **domestic** guinea pig. There are even more crossbreeds. Crossbreed guinea pigs are born to parents that are of two or more different breeds. Purebred guinea pigs have parents of the same breed. Knowing the different types of guinea pigs will help you to choose your perfect pet.

AMERICAN

- Most popular breed for pet owners
- Short, smooth coat
- Easy to **groom**
- Grows to be 10 to 14 inches in length
- Also known as the English Cavy

ABYSSINIAN

- Short, wiry coat
- Hair grows in spiral **tufts** called rosettes
- Most have five to ten rosettes
- Ridge along the spine
- Does not like to be handled as much as smooth-haired guinea pigs
- Mustache around the nose

PERUVIAN

- Long, smooth coat
- Hair parts down the middle of the back and grows over the sides, rump, head, and face
- Needs to be groomed quite often
- Hair grows up to 20 inches long

Guinea pigs come in a variety of colors. Guinea pigs with coats of one color are called self types. Non-self, or marked, types can have up to three colors in their coats. Aside from different coat colors, guinea pigs also have different hairstyles. Some have hair that is long and silky. Others have short and wiry coats. Some even have hair that grows in tufts all over their bodies.

SILKIE

- Long, silky coat that grows 8 to 10 inches long
- Head and face are not covered with hair
- Also known as a sheltie
- Baby silkies look like American guinea pigs

TEDDY

- Popular pet in the United States
- Short, dense coat that sticks out from the body
- Fur bounces back up when patted down
- Easy to groom
- Large, bright eyes

WHITE CRESTED

- Short, smooth coat
- Single, white rosette on top of the head
- Large, bold eyes
- Roman nose, which is a nose that is higher than normal at the top

Crazy for Cavies

Guinea pigs come from South America, where they have lived in the wild for thousands of years. South American Native Peoples called Incas were **taming** and breeding wild guinea pigs as early as 9000 BC. In the 1500s, European sailors began arriving in South America. Some of these sailors took guinea pigs back home to Europe. Soon, people in many parts of Europe wanted to keep guinea pigs as pets. At first, guinea pigs were very expensive. Only rich people or royalty could afford to buy these furry friends. However, as time passed, guinea pigs became more affordable. When Europeans began to settle in North America, they brought their pet guinea pigs with them.

■ Guinea pigs can be taught tricks. Some will even come when their name is called.

It is not known how guinea pigs got their name. Guinea pigs do not come from Guinea, Africa, and they do not look like pigs. Some people believe that guinea pigs were given the guinea part of their name by Spanish sailors. The sailors sold guinea pigs for one gold coin, known as a guinea. Stories also say that the animals were given the pig part of their name because they squeal like pigs.

Do not put any plastic items in your guinea pig's hutch. Your pet may chew the plastic and swallow pieces she cannot digest.

■ Guinea pigs were the first rodents to be domesticated.

Fascinating Facts

- Wild cavies still live in the grasslands and mountains of South America. As many as 10 wild cavies live together in burrows, or underground homes. They search for food at night.
- If a wild guinea pig is being chased by a **predator**, she might pretend to be dead.

Life Cycle

Guinea pigs have a life span of 5 to 8 years. With proper care, some guinea pigs can live even longer. A guinea pig has different needs at different stages of his life. At all stages of life, a guinea pig will depend on his owner for love and attention.

Newborn Guinea Pigs

Newborn guinea pigs are called puppies. Unlike newborn hamsters or rabbits, puppies have fur. In fact, they look like smaller versions of their parents. Puppies are born with their eyes open and have a full set of teeth. Within a few days, puppies are able to walk and nibble food.

Mature Guinea Pigs

Guinea pigs mature at different times. As guinea pigs start to age, their coats become dull, and they begin to lose hair. Mature guinea pigs will sleep more and play less. Guinea pigs who have reached maturity are more likely to develop illnesses.

Fascinating Facts

- A mother guinea pig is pregnant for about 70 days. This is a long time compared to other rodents. In nature, guinea pigs are born in the open, with little to protect them from danger. Puppies need to be quite developed at birth so they can protect themselves against predators.

Three to Five Weeks

Guinea pigs stop drinking their mother's milk when they are about 3 weeks old. They are very playful and curious. Young guinea pigs can have babies. However, they are too young to make good parents. To prevent young guinea pigs from mating, the males and females should be kept apart.

Adulthood

By 5 or 6 months of age, guinea pigs are fully grown. Both male and female guinea pigs are now mature enough to take care of babies. Adult guinea pigs are active and social. They like to be kept busy. For example, guinea pigs like to play with old socks, shoe boxes, tennis balls, and plumbing pipe.

Picking Your Pet

Choosing a guinea pig is a big responsibility. There are many things to consider before selecting a new pet. The following questions will help you to decide what type of guinea pig is right for you.

Which Type of Guinea Pig Should I Get?

All guinea pigs, no matter what their breed, are friendly and easy to handle. Probably the most important thing to consider when choosing a pet is how much time you want to spend grooming his coat. Breeds with smooth, short coats are the easiest to keep clean and well groomed. Longhaired guinea pigs, such as Peruvians or silkies, need much more time and attention. Their long coats require brushing and cleaning every day, and their fur must be trimmed quite often.

Try to choose a guinea pig that is about 6 weeks old. Young guinea pigs are easier to tame.

■ Abyssinians need to be groomed more often than American guinea pigs.

American

Abyssinian

Guinea pigs are social animals. They enjoy living with one or two other guinea pigs.

Where Can I Buy a Pet Guinea Pig?

The most common place to buy a guinea pig is a pet store. Pet stores usually sell crossbred guinea pigs. If you want to purchase a purebred guinea pig, you will probably have to go to a private **breeder**. Breeders know much about the guinea pigs they raise. They will be able to provide information and tips about how to care for your new pet. You may also be able to get a guinea pig at a local animal shelter. Often, animal shelters have many older guinea pigs in need of good homes.

What Should I Look for When I Am Picking My Guinea Pig?

Try to choose a guinea pig that is in good health. A healthy guinea pig should be plump. His coat should be shiny and free of bald spots. He should be alert and curious, and his eyes should be bright and clear. His nose should be dry, and his ears should be clean.

Fascinating Facts

- A male guinea pig is called a boar, and a female guinea pig is called a sow.
- An average sow weighs about 2 pounds. Boars weigh slightly more than sows.

Guinea Pig Gear

Moving to a new home can be stressful for any animal. To help make your guinea pig feel more comfortable, it is a good idea to be prepared with some basic equipment. The most important item your new pet will need is a cage or a hutch. Most pet stores sell large guinea pig cages. However, many people believe that a wooden hutch is a better house for a guinea pig. A wooden hutch usually has more space than a wire cage. Whatever kind of house you choose, make sure that it has proper **ventilation** and a solid bottom. It should also have separate areas for playing and sleeping.

Do not put cedar wood shavings inside your pet's cage. Cedar is toxic to guinea pigs.

Guinea pigs need special toys inside their cages to keep them from becoming bored.

Your pet guinea pig will settle nicely into his new home if you make the space as comfortable as possible. The floor of the hutch should be covered with **absorbent** wood shavings. Your pet can **burrow** in these shavings. Be sure to provide your guinea pig with plenty of bedding material, too. Wood shavings, hay, and straw can be used for bedding. The hutch should also have a large water bottle, a piece of wood for **gnawing**, and a food bowl that will not tip over.

■ Be sure to store hay and straw properly so that it does not grow mold.

Fascinating Facts

- Guinea pigs are happiest and healthiest in places where the temperature is above 65 degrees Fahrenheit.
- Guinea pigs can be trained to use a litter box.

Guinea Pigging Out

Guinea pigs are herbivores, which means that they only eat plant matter. There is no meat in their diets. The best way to ensure that your pet guinea pig is getting the proper **nutrition** is to give her guinea pig feed pellets. These pellets are available at most pet stores and at many supermarkets. Your guinea pig should also be given fresh fruits and vegetables every day, as well as plenty of hay.

Leftover fruits and vegetables can rot if they are not removed from the cage each day.

■ Wash all fruits and vegetables before feeding them to your guinea pig. Even small amounts of dirt can make her ill.

It is important to feed your guinea pig twice a day. Try to feed your pet at the same time each day. Guinea pigs are creatures of habit. They like a set routine, and they look forward to their mealtimes.

When you first get your guinea pig, ask a **veterinarian** or a breeder how much food to give your pet. Be sure to provide your guinea pig with a constant supply of water, too. A guinea pig should never be without fresh, clean water.

■ Plastic sipper bottles with stainless steel tips work well for providing water to guinea pigs.

Fascinating Facts

- Just like humans, guinea pigs are unable to produce vitamin C in their own bodies. Without enough vitamin C, guinea pigs are likely to develop an illness called **scurvy**. To prevent scurvy, be sure to give your pet fresh foods that are rich in vitamin C, including broccoli, carrots, cauliflower, and oranges.

From Feet to Fur

Although guinea pig types look different, they have many of the same features. All guinea pigs have similar sizes and weights. They all have plump, round bodies, short tails, and fragile skeletons. They also have thick necks to support their large heads. Guinea pigs have large stomachs that allow them to digest their **vegetarian** meals easily. They also have short legs so that they never have to crouch down far to pick up food.

- AMERICAN

Guinea pigs have three toes on their back feet and four toes on their front feet. Each foot has sharp claws and leathery soles, or pads, that cover the bottom. These pads help protect the animal's fragile toe bones.

Guinea pigs have a good sense of hearing. They are able to hear high-pitched sounds much better than humans. Most guinea pigs are able to recognize other guinea pigs by the sounds they make.

Guinea pigs have large, glossy eyes located on the sides of their head. Guinea pigs can see colors. They are also able to see more images per second than humans. A guinea pig sees 33 images per second, while a human sees an average of 20 images per second.

Guinea pigs have a keen sense of smell. They use their little pink noses to sniff out danger.

Guinea pigs have twenty teeth. Their teeth are open-rooted, which means that they never stop growing. Guinea pigs use their sharp front teeth to bite and gnaw their food.

The whiskers on a guinea pig's face are quite long, like a cat's whiskers. Guinea pigs use their whiskers to find objects in the dark.

Keeping Clean

Guinea pigs are very clean animals. They are happiest when their home is neat and tidy. To help keep a guinea pig happy and healthy, the owner should clean his cage daily. When cleaning a guinea pig's cage, droppings and soiled bedding should be removed, and the feeding equipment should be washed. Remember to put fresh bedding, food, and water in the cage.

Your guinea pig's home will need a more thorough cleaning once a week. To do this, take everything out of the cage and scrub it with hot, soapy water or a mild cleanser that is safe for animals. Make sure the cage is rinsed well and completely dry before putting in fresh shavings and bedding.

Use a soft baby brush or a toothbrush when grooming your guinea pig. Brushes with harder bristles may scratch and harm your pet's skin.

■ Do not use cat litter in a guinea pig's litter box. Fragrances, dust, and hard pieces may harm him.

Guinea pigs also like to look their best. Most guinea pigs groom themselves regularly. They use their front paws and teeth as combs and their tongue as a washcloth. Although most guinea pigs keep themselves clean, owners should help with their grooming. Smooth-haired breeds should be brushed once a week. Breeds with rough or long coats need to be brushed and combed every day.

■■ At first, guinea pigs do not like to be brushed. Be gentle and take care not to pull his fur. Soon, your guinea pig will learn to enjoy being groomed.

Fascinating Facts

- Guinea pigs file their teeth by gnawing on wood. Always be sure to have a piece of gnawing wood in your pet's cage. If your guinea pig's teeth are too long or uneven, a veterinarian will have to clip them. A veterinarian can also clip your pet's claws.

Healthy and Happy

Guinea pigs are usually healthy animals. If they receive proper care, they rarely become ill. To keep your guinea pig in top shape, feed her a balanced diet. You need to groom her and clean out her hutch regularly, too. Guinea pigs are nervous pets, and they scare easily. This can be harmful to their health. Loud noises and too much handling are common sources of stress for guinea pigs. To avoid scaring your pet, always speak softly and do not let too many people handle her. Keep her hutch in a quiet place where she will not be frightened by sudden noises or other pets.

Examine your pet's coat every day to make sure it is free of lice and mites.

■ Guinea pigs need a safe place to hide when they are scared or stressed.

Sometimes, even if a guinea pig is given proper care, she may become ill. Whenever you are handling your guinea pig, give her a quick health check. Your guinea pig might be sick if she is eating less food, exercising less often, or has wetness around her eyes and nose. If you notice any of these **symptoms**, take your guinea pig to a veterinarian right away.

■ Ask a local animal shelter for the name of a veterinarian who has experience with guinea pigs.

Fascinating Facts

- Guinea pigs can catch colds from drafts, dampness, or temperature changes.
- Guinea pigs need to exercise. Many owners let their guinea pigs run free in the house or garden. Owners must be sure to watch their guinea pig closely when she is outdoors. Others build an exercise run, which is a long cage that can be placed on the floor or on the ground outside.

Cavy Comfort

When owners first bring their guinea pig home, he will probably be nervous and shy. New owners may want to play with their new pet right away. It is best to leave him alone for a while. Quietly watch your guinea pig as he explores and settles into his hutch. After a day or two, spend some time talking softly to your pet so he will get to know your voice. Let another day pass before offering your guinea pig food from your hand. Once he is comfortable being fed by hand, you can try to hold him.

Be sure to keep your pet's cage away from the television or stereo. Loud noises scare guinea pigs.

■ Give your guinea pig time to adjust to his new home before trying to hold him.

Pet Peeves

Guinea pigs do not like:
- loud noises
- having their fur ruffled
- too much attention
- too little attention
- being too hot or too cold
- straw bedding instead of hay

When you are ready to pick up your guinea pig, approach him from the front so he is able to see you coming. Move slowly to avoid startling him. Pick up your guinea pig gently, placing one hand around his shoulders and the other under his bottom. Hold your pet for a short time at first. Each day, slowly increase the amount of time you spend handling your guinea pig. After a while, your guinea pig will be happy to see you approaching.

■ Guinea pigs must be held properly. If they become scared and struggle to get free, they might fall and hurt themselves.

Fascinating Facts

- Guinea pigs enjoy using their voices. When they are content, they make a variety of noises, including gurgles, grunts, and squeaks.
- On occasion, you may see your guinea pig jump high into the air. This jumping is called "popcorning," and it is the sign of a happy, healthy guinea pig.

Best in Show

Humans have been raising and breeding guinea pigs for thousands of years. At first, early South Americans tamed wild guinea pigs to use as a source of food. As time passed, people all over the world began to realize that guinea pigs made better pets than meals. Today, guinea pigs are very popular animals. Not only are they kept as pets, some have even appeared in films and television shows. One of the best-known cavy stars is GP the Guinea Pig. He is the clever inventor on the television show *Hammy the Hamster*.

Rabbit cages do not make good guinea pig hutches. Since guinea pigs do not have fur on their feet, they will get sores from the wire floor.

■ GP the Guinea Pig is one of the stars of the television show *Hammy the Hamster*.

Fascinating Facts

- Guinea pigs can be taught tricks. With the right treats and plenty of patience, you can teach your guinea pig to waltz, jump, and turn in a circle.
- Guinea pigs were among the first small **mammals** to be sent to outer space.

A popular hobby for many guinea pig owners is entering their pets into shows. Cavy shows and competitions are held all over the world. Prizes are given to the best guinea pig handler at these competitions. The judges follow a set of guidelines, or rules, that help them select a winner. If you wish to show your pet, join a local cavy club and attend as many shows as possible.

■ The American Cavy Breeders Association can provide information about guinea pig shows.

Guinea Pig Tales

In *Jenius: The Amazing Guinea Pig*, Judy has two pet guinea pigs named Molly and Joe. One day, Molly gives birth to a baby guinea pig. Judy names the baby Jenius. Jenius is a very smart guinea pig. He can perform many tricks, such as sit, stay, and play dead. Judy wants to prove that guinea pigs are smarter than people think. She takes Jenius to school for show-and-tell, but he does not perform his tricks. Now, Judy must find another way to prove Jenius has talent.

From Dave King-Smith's *Jenius: The Amazing Guinea Pig*

Pet Puzzlers

How much do you know about guinea pigs? If you can answer the following questions correctly, you may be ready to own a pet guinea pig.

Q How many years do guinea pigs live?

Guinea pigs usually live to be 5 to 8 years old.

Q How often should a guinea pig be fed?

Most veterinarians say that a pet guinea pig should be fed twice each day. If possible, owners should also try to feed their pet at the same time each day.

Q Why do guinea pigs need a piece of gnawing wood in their cage or hutch?

Guinea pigs use gnawing wood to file their front teeth.

Q How often should guinea pigs be groomed?

A smooth-haired guinea pig should be groomed once a week. A rough or longhaired guinea pig should be groomed every day.

Q What is popcorning?

Popcorning is the term used to describe when a guinea pig jumps high in the air. Popcorning is a sign of a happy guinea pig.

Q Do guinea pigs see in black and white or in color?

Guinea pigs see in color. They especially like the color green.

Q What are some signs that a guinea pig is sick?

A guinea pig might be sick if she is eating less food, exercising less often, or has wetness around her eyes and nose.

Calling Your Cavy

Before you buy your pet guinea pig, write down some guinea pig names that you like. Some names may work better for a female guinea pig. Others may suit a male guinea pig. Here are just a few suggestions:

Popcorn

Arnold

Trixie

Porky

Barney

Patches

Ginger

Lucy

Lady

Rex

Frequently Asked Questions

Should I get more than one guinea pig?

Guinea pigs are very social animals. In nature, they live in groups of five to ten. Pet guinea pigs are happiest and healthiest when they have at least one cavy companion. If you decide to keep only one guinea pig as a pet, be sure to give him plenty of attention.

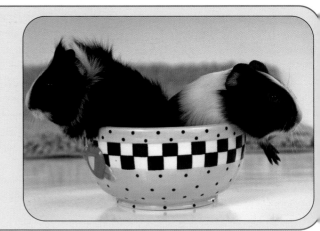

Should I breed my guinea pigs?

Breeding guinea pigs is a big responsibility. You should think carefully before putting a male and a female together. A female guinea pig can have a litter of four puppies. The mother will care for her puppies for the first few weeks following the births. After that, it will be your responsibility to care for the young guinea pigs.

Should I keep my guinea pig's hutch inside or outside?

If you live in a mild climate, you can let your guinea pig live outside for most of the year. Be sure to position the hutch in a place that is protected from direct sunlight, drafts, and bad weather. The hutch should be raised off the ground, and it should have strong door latches. This will help keep your guinea pig from getting out, and it will keep other animals from getting in. Guinea pigs do not like weather that is too cold or too hot. When the weather gets too extreme, be sure to bring your pet inside.

More Information

Animal Organizations

You can help guinea pigs stay happy and healthy by learning more about them. Many organizations are dedicated to teaching people how to care for and protect their pet pals. For more guinea pig information, write to the following organizations:

American Cavy Breeders Association
P.O. Box 876392
Wasilla, AK 99687

American Rabbit Breeders Association
P.O. Box 426
Bloomington, IL 61702

Web Sites

To answer more of your guinea pig questions, go online and surf to the following Web sites:

Animal Adventure Pets
www.animaladventurepets.com

Pets Hub
www.petshub.com/guinea-pigs

Pet Place
www.petplace.com

Words to Know

absorbent: able to soak up moisture
breeder: a person who raises specific types of animals or plants
breeds: groups of animals that share certain characteristics
burrow: to dig a hole
domestic: tamed and used to living among people; not living in the wild
gnawing: wearing away by nonstop biting or chewing
groom: cleaning by removing dirt and tangles from fur
mammals: warm-blooded animals that have hair and drink their mother's milk
nutrition: the proper food needed for health

predator: an animal that hunts and kills other animals for food
scurvy: a disease that causes loose teeth, bruises, bleeding gums, and muscle pain
symptoms: signs of illness
taming: to change from living in the wild to living among people
temperaments: personalities
tufts: clumps or clusters
vegetarian: an animal that does not eat meat or fish
ventilation: constant fresh air
veterinarian: animal doctor

Index